Transcending Race in America
Biographies of Biracial Achievers

Halle Berry

Beyoncé

David Blaine

Mariah Carey

Frederick Douglass

W. E. B. Du Bois

Salma Hayek

Derek Jeter

Alicia Keys

Soledad O'Brien

Rosa Parks

Prince

Booker T. Washington

BOOKER T. WASHINGTON

Educator, Author, and Civil Rights Leader

Jim Whiting

Mason Crest Publishers

Produced by 21st Century Publishing and Communications, Inc.

MASON CREST PUBLISHERS INC.
370 Reed Road
Broomall, Pennsylvania 19008
(866) MCP-BOOK (toll free)
www.masoncrest.com

Printed in the United States of America.

First Printing

9 8 7 6 5 4 3 2 1

Library of Congress Cataloging-in-Publication Data

Whiting, Jim, 1943–
    Booker T. Washington / Jim Whiting.
       p. cm. — (Transcending race in America: biographies of biracial achievers)
    Includes bibliographical references and index.
    ISBN 978-1-4222-1608-8 (hardback : alk. paper) — ISBN 978-1-4222-1622-4 (pbk. : alk. paper)
    1. Washington, Booker T., 1856–1915—Juvenile literature. 2. African Americans—Biography—Juvenile literature. 3. Educators—United States—Biography—Juvenile literature. I. Title.
E185.97.W4W48 2010
370.92—dc22
[B]   2009027039

Publisher's notes:
All quotations in this book come from original sources, and contain the spelling and grammatical inconsistencies of the original text.

The Web sites mentioned in this book were active at the time of publication. The publisher is not responsible for Web sites that have changed their addresses or discontinued operation since the date of publication. The publisher will review and update the Web site addresses each time the book is reprinted.

Table of Contents

> **"I** have brothers, sisters, nieces, nephews, uncles, and cousins, of every race and every hue, scattered across three continents, and for as long as I live, I will never forget that in no other country on Earth is my story even possible. **"**

> **"We** may have different stories, but we hold common hopes. . . . We may not look the same and we may not have come from the same place, but we all want to move in the same direction — towards a better future . . . **"**

— Barack Obama, 44th President of the United States of America

1

Taking a Chance

IN 1881, BOOKER T. WASHINGTON BECAME the first black man in U.S. history to be a school principal. The Alabama state legislature had just voted to establish a new school for blacks in the town of Tuskegee. Booker's drive and determination eventually made what is now Tuskegee University into one of the country's leading black schools.

Tuskegee is one of over 100 historically black colleges and universities (HBCU) in the United States. Like Tuskegee, many were established soon after the Civil War.

It would be very difficult to find a school anywhere in the United States as closely connected to its founder as Tuskegee is to Booker. He was just 25 when he was named as principal. He didn't have much experience in education. He never took any formal courses in teaching. He had taught only a few years.

Booker T. Washington was a young, inexperienced teacher when he took a chance and established what is now Tuskegee University. His dedication and drive turned a small school with no buildings or resources into one of America's leading black colleges.

Alabama State University

Another notable HBCU is Alabama State University, located in the state capital of Montgomery. The school was founded in 1867 as Lincoln Normal School by nine freed slaves.

Seven years later it was the first black college in the United States to receive official state financial support. In 1878 William Paterson became president of the college. He served for 37 years and was as important in developing the school as Booker was at Tuskegee.

The school went through several name changes in the 1900s. It became Alabama State University in 1954. Today the school serves more than 5,000 students.

SOMETHING COMPLETELY DIFFERENT

Booker was also breaking new ground. If a white man had been appointed principal of Tuskegee, everyone would assume the school would be successful. Many people doubted that a black man was up to the task. Booker knew he was "on trial":

> **"We were trying an experiment—that of testing whether or not it was possible for Negroes to build up and control the affairs of a large educational institution. If we failed it would injure the entire race."**

Booker literally had to build Tuskegee from the ground up. When he arrived, the school didn't even have a site. So his first task was to buy land. Then he had to start putting up buildings. All this meant many long hours of hard physical work and trying to persuade people to donate money. But starting from scratch gave Booker one big advantage. He could do things his own way.

To Booker, his own way reflected his own life experience. As he wrote,

> **"There was no period of my life that was devoted to play. From the time that I can remember anything, almost every day of my life has been occupied in some kind of labour."**

To Booker, this wasn't a bad thing. While attending Hampton Normal and Agricultural Institute in the mid-1870s, he had worked his way through school. When he graduated, he wrote he had "learned to love labour, not alone for its financial value, but for labour's own sake and for the independence and self-reliance which the ability to do something which the world wants brings."

THE VALUE OF HARD WORK

Hard work, he felt, taught key values such as self-discipline, morality, and the importance of helping other people. He knew that developing his "love of labour" among Tuskegee students

Tuskegee students dig the foundation for a campus building. Booker had to start from scratch, putting up buildings and fundraising for the school. He felt he and the school were being tested to see if blacks could succeed in running a college.

wouldn't be an easy process. During the long era of slavery, blacks "had been compelled to work for two hundred and fifty years, and now they wanted their children to go to school so that they might be free and live like the white folks—without working," he wrote.

An unwillingness to work wasn't the only issue Booker faced:

> **"The students who came first seemed to be fond of memorizing long and complicated 'rules' in grammar and mathematics, but had little thought or knowledge of applying these rules to the everyday affairs of their lives."**

Booker works in his office at Tuskegee. He had learned the value of hard work and wanted others to see its value, too. He was tireless in his efforts to convince students that learning a trade would help them get along in the white world.

Booker knew that attitude had to change. He believed "everyday affairs" were very important. His students needed to learn personal cleanliness, to care for their teeth and clothing. They needed to learn how to set a table, how to eat in the company of others, and how to keep their rooms neat and clean.

Above all, he wrote:

> **"We wanted to give them such a practical knowledge of some one industry, together with the spirit of industry, thrift, and economy, that they would be sure of knowing how to make a living after they had left us. We wanted to teach them to study actual things instead of mere books alone."**

Over the years, Booker would encounter many obstacles. But he always believed he was right:

> **"The individual who can do something that the world wants done will, in the end, make his way regardless of his race. . . . My experience is that there is something in human nature which always makes an individual recognize and reward merit, no matter under what colour of skin merit is found . . . it is the visible, the tangible that goes a long way in softening prejudices."**

As events would prove, Booker was not entirely correct. Many whites didn't like it when blacks succeeded. But Booker never lost sight of his goal. Up to within a few hours of his death, he was working to improve both Tuskegee and educational opportunities for all blacks.

2

Getting
an Education

BOOKER T. WASHINGTON WAS BORN IN 1856 in Virginia as a slave. For years, Booker thought he was born in 1858 or 1859. Later evidence showed his birthdate was actually April 5, 1856.

One thing is certain. Booker was born into slavery. He belonged to James Burroughs, who owned a 200-acre farm in Virginia. In a way, Booker was lucky. Burroughs treated his slaves decently. Sometimes he and his sons worked beside the slaves in the fields.

Booker's mother was Jane Ferguson. She was a slave who was the farm's cook.

His father's identity is unknown, though the man must have been white. Booker had light skin, reddish hair, and gray eyes. Booker said not knowing his father didn't bother him:

66 **Whoever he was, I never heard of his taking the least interest in me or providing in any way for my**

Elizabeth and James Burroughs owned the Virginia farm where Booker was born into slavery. Being a slave was a terrible life, and Booker always looked for ways to better himself. When he saw the Burroughs daughters go to school, he realized the value of getting an education.

Slavery in America

Black slaves arrived In the United States just a few years after English settlers founded the Jamestown colony in 1607. Slavery spread throughout the colonies, though most slaves worked in the southern states.

Slaves were the legal property of their white owners. They had almost no rights. Slave owners often bought and sold them. Families were frequently broken up.

The northern states began **abolishing** slavery in the late 1700s. But it kept growing in the southern states. Disagreement about slavery between North and South was one of the main causes of the Civil War. Slavery finally came to an end when the Thirteenth Amendment to the U.S. Constitution was **ratified** in December, 1865.

rearing. But I do not find especial fault with him. He was simply another unfortunate victim of the institution [slavery] which the Nation unhappily had **engrafted** upon it at that time.❞

Booker's living conditions were primitive. The tiny cabin had no windows and was drafty. Booker and his family slept on the dirt floor. They didn't have much to eat.

Booker grew up in this tiny cabin, which is now part of the Booker T. Washington National Monument in Franklin County, Virginia. The son of a slave woman and an unknown white father, Booker lived in the primitive house and worked hard every day, often not getting enough to eat.

ALWAYS A WORKER

From an early age, Booker had to work. He helped clean the house and carried water to workers in the fields. He shooed flies away from the Burroughs family while they ate.

Booker had glimpses of a better life when he carried school books for the Burroughs daughters. As a slave, he couldn't attend school. Some slaves, such as the famous **orator** and editor Frederick Douglass, still managed to become educated.

Frederick Douglass

Frederick Douglass was born a slave in 1818. He escaped 20 years later and settled in the North. He soon became a famous speaker, describing the evils of slavery. His 1845 autobiography made him even more famous.

He began publishing an anti-slavery newspaper called the *North Star* in 1847.

When the Civil War began, he was the best-known black man in the country. He helped convince President Abraham Lincoln to issue the Emancipation Proclamation, which freed the slaves, and to let black men serve as soldiers.

He continued to speak out on black issues for the rest of his life. He died in 1895.

What Booker saw of school made a deep impression:

> **"I had the feeling that to get into a schoolhouse and study in this way would be about the same as getting into paradise."**

Booker's chance to "get into paradise" began in 1865 when the Civil War ended. Several years earlier his mother had married Washington Ferguson, a slave on a nearby farm, even though they lived apart. Ferguson escaped and fled to Malden, West Virginia. With the war over, Mary took her family there.

Ferguson put Booker to work in a salt factory. When a school for blacks opened, Booker wanted to attend. Ferguson said no. The family needed his earnings. Booker didn't give up so easily, and persisted in his requests. Finally Ferguson said Booker could take lessons at night.

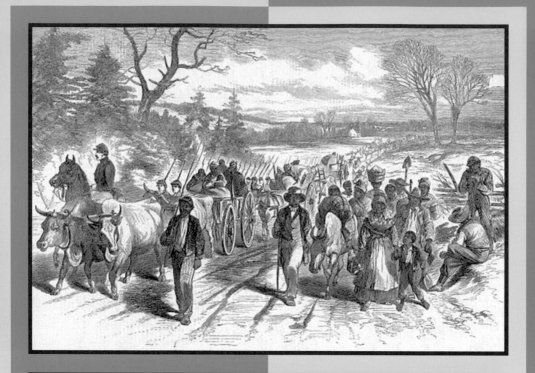

Free slaves travel to the North to seek a better life after the Civil War. Booker and his family moved to West Virginia after the war. There he attended a school for blacks and dreamed of furthering his education at Hampton Institute.

Booker still wanted to attend during the day. Ferguson said if he got up at 4:00 in the morning and worked several hours, he could go. Then he had to work after school.

MAKING HIS OWN NAME

On the first day, the teacher asked Booker for his full name. Booker was confused. He had never been anything but "Booker." Impulsively, he said "Booker Washington," after his stepfather's first name. Later his mother said she had named him Booker Taliaferro when he was born. He began calling himself Booker T. Washington, which pleased him:

> **"I think there are not many men in country who have had the privilege of naming themselves in the way that I have."**

Working and going to school was too exhausting. Booker returned to his lessons at night. Sometimes he had to walk several miles in the darkness. Quitting wasn't an option:

> **"There was never a time in my youth, no matter how dark and discouraging the days might be, when one resolve did not continually remain with me, and that was a determination to secure an education at any cost."**

Soon Booker's days literally became dark. Ferguson got him a job in a coal mine. Booker dreaded each day. The work was filthy, frightening, and dangerous.

HEARING ABOUT A SCHOOL

Working in the coal mine had one priceless benefit. One day Booker overheard two miners talking about a school for blacks in Virginia. It was the Hampton Normal and Agricultural Institute, and it immediately fired his imagination:

> **"As they went on describing the school, it seemed to me that it must be the greatest place on earth. . . . I resolved at once to go to that school, although I had no idea where it was, or how many miles away, or how I was going to reach it; I remembered only that I was on fire constantly with one ambition, and that was to go to Hampton."**

Then he got a houseboy job with Lewis Ruffner, who owned the salt factory and coal mine. Viola Ruffner, Ruffner's wife, was very demanding. "She wanted everything kept clean about her. . . . Nothing must be **sloven** or slipshod; every door, every fence, must be kept in repair," Booker wrote.

When Mrs. Ruffner realized that Booker met her high standards, she encouraged his desire for more education and often gave him lessons herself. She taught him how to speak well and urged him to pay particular attention to personal cleanliness.

"The lessons that I learned in the home of Mrs. Ruffner were as valuable to me as any education I have ever gotten anywhere since," Booker wrote.

GOING TO HAMPTON

In 1872, Booker was ready to realize his Hampton dream. He only had a few dollars for a journey of several hundred miles. Though that money soon ran out, Booker was determined to continue. He was often hungry and one night even slept under a wooden sidewalk.

But Booker's first glimpse of the school made the hardships all worthwhile:

> **"I felt that I had reached the promised land, and I resolved to let no obstacle prevent me from putting forth the highest effort to fit myself to accomplish the most good in the world."**

No one was expecting Booker. He didn't look very impressive after a long trip in the same clothes without being able to wash up. His education from Mrs. Ruffner saved him. After interviewing Booker, the head teacher handed him a broom and told him to clean a nearby room. He realized it was a kind of entrance examination. Booker gave it his best shot:

> **"I swept the recitation room three times. Then I got a dusting-cloth and dusted it four times. All the woodwork around the walls, every bench, table and desk, I went over four times with my dusting-cloth."**

Using a white handkerchief, the teacher couldn't find a speck of dirt. Booker said, "I have passed several examinations since then, but I have always felt that this was the best one I ever passed."

Soon Booker met the school's founder, Samuel Armstrong. Armstrong was a white man who had founded the school four years earlier to meet a huge demand for education by blacks.

Armstrong ran the school like a military camp. The students rose early in the morning, marched to their classes, prayed at regular times, and had daily clothing inspections.

In spite of the intense discipline, Armstrong "was worshipped by his students," Booker said. "I do not hesitate to say that I have never met any man who, in my estimation, was the equal of General Armstrong."

Students learn about the solar system in a class at the Hampton Institute in Virginia. When Booker finally arrived at Hampton, a teacher asked him to clean a room. He worked hard to impress the woman, who let him into the school because he had made the room spotlessly clean.

Samuel Armstrong

Samuel Armstrong was born in Hawaii in 1839 and came to Massachusetts to attend college in 1860. He became an officer in the Union army two years later and fought at the Battle of Gettysburg in 1863.

Soon afterward he took command of a regiment of black soldiers, eventually becoming a general. His experiences with the regiment interested him in black issues. He became convinced that education was the best way of dealing with the problems that arose after the war, and soon he founded Hampton.

Armstrong devoted the rest of his life to the school. He became paralyzed in 1892 and died the following year.

Armstrong believed that blacks were inferior to whites at this point in history because of the negative effects of slavery. He thought it was up to whites like himself to help blacks regain the sense of morality and personal responsibility that slavery had destroyed.

PASSING ON THE VALUE OF HARD WORK

As a result, the main emphasis at Hampton was in training teachers who would pass on the school's values to their students. Chief among those values was hard work. Working hard led to success and social advancement. While students learned some history, math, and similar subjects, they spent most of their time in gaining knowledge of useful trades such as farming, carpentry, cooking, and tailoring. That way they could fit into the larger society around them.

From the moment he arrived, Booker lived up to Armstrong's expectations. Because of his lack of money, he took a job as a janitor to cover his expenses:

> **"I was determined from the first to make my work as janitor so valuable that my services would be indispensable. This I succeeded in doing to such an extent that I was soon informed that I would be allowed the full cost of my board in return for my work."**

He took a vacation from Hampton after his second year and went home. His mother died during this time, which greatly saddened

Samuel Armstrong, the founder and head of Hampton Institute, believed in the value of hard work as a route to success. He felt his job was to help blacks recover the sense of responsibility they had lost during slavery. Armstrong devoted his life to Hampton and was a trusted mentor to Booker.

As a young college graduate, Booker returned to his hometown and taught there for three years. He began a night school and also gave private lessons. He even emphasized civility that went beyond "book learning," including the use of the toothbrush.

him. Booker returned to Hampton and graduated in 1875. He had done so well that he was invited to speak to his graduating class.

GIVING BACK TO HIS HOMETOWN

He went back to Malden and taught for three years. From the start, he made it clear that "mere book education was not all that the young people of that town needed." He was particularly emphatic that they master one "educational tool":

> **"In all my teaching I have watched carefully the influence of the tooth-brush, and I am convinced that there are few single agencies of civilization that are more far-reaching."**

He began a night school because so many people worked during the day. He also organized a debating society and gave private lessons. As a result, he typically began his days at 8:00 in the morning and worked until 10:00 at night.

After three years of teaching, Booker began attending Wayland Baptist Theological Seminary in Washington, D.C. Apparently he thought about becoming a minister, though he left after less than a year. He didn't say much about his experience there, apart from his opinion that his fellow students paid too much attention "to mere outward appearances."

Soon afterward, Armstrong invited Booker to address the 1879 graduating class at Hampton. The speech went well, and several months later Armstrong offered the young man a teaching job at Hampton. Booker probably would have remained there for a long time.

But unknown to him, late the following year two men had a meeting several hundred miles away. That meeting would completely change the direction of Booker's life and set the stage for his enduring fame.

Chapter
3

❦

Putting Tuskegee on the Map

IN 1880, W.F. FOSTER, A FORMER SLAVE OWNER and Confederate army officer, ran for the Alabama legislature. To win, Foster needed black votes. He met with Lewis Adams, the most prominent black man in the town of Tuskegee. Meanwhile, Adams had wanted to establish a school for blacks in Tuskegee.

The two men made a deal. In exchange for receiving the town's black vote, Foster would support a college for blacks there.

THE DEAL IS SEALED

Both men kept their word. Adams encouraged enough black voters to elect Foster. Foster immediately introduced a bill to provide $2,000 for the school. Adams and George Campbell, a local banker, wrote letters to various institutions seeking a white man to run the school. One of the letters went to Armstrong, who said he didn't know any whites who would be interested. But he recommended

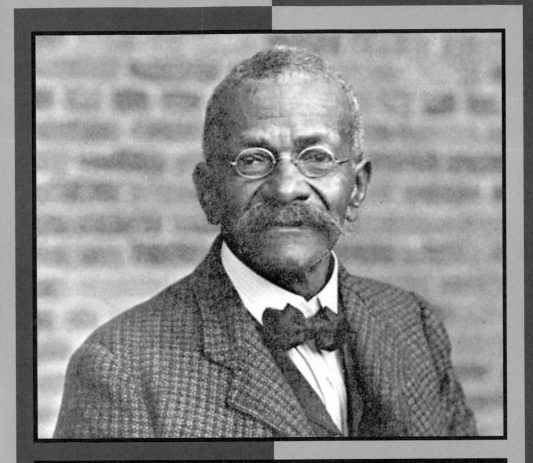

Lewis Adams, a former slave turned successful businessman, dreamed of establishing a black college in Tuskegee, Alabama. He and a local legislator helped make the dream a reality. Although they first looked for a white administrator, Booker's mentor, Samuel Armstrong, recommended Booker to run the school.

"a very competent capable **mulatto**, clear headed, modest, sensible, polite and thorough teacher and superior man."

Armstrong was, of course, referring to Booker. Several days later, he received a telegram: "Booker T. Washington will suit us. Send him at once."

Booker shows his eagerness in this early portrait. He was excited to go to Alabama to further the education of black students who were hungry for knowledge. But on arriving at Tuskegee, he was surprised that he had to start from zero, including buying land and building classrooms.

Booker received a stunning surprise on his arrival in late June:

> **"I had expected to find there a building and all the necessary apparatus ready for me to begin teaching. To my disappointment, I found nothing of the kind."**

HUNGRY FOR KNOWLEDGE

On the other hand, he found "hundreds of hungry, earnest souls who wanted to secure knowledge."

Booker wanted to satisfy this hunger as soon as possible. His first task was finding a place to hold classes. This task was more difficult because the money from the legislature was only for teacher salaries. There wasn't a penny for land or buildings.

A church let him use "a rather **dilapidated** shanty" that was "in about as bad condition as possible," Booker wrote. Classes began July 4. Booker was the only teacher.

His first weeks were a whirlwind of activity. Besides teaching, he made friends—both black and white—in Tuskegee, traveled through the countryside recruiting students, and looked for a permanent site for the school.

His energy soon paid off. Olivia Davidson joined him as the school's second teacher. She shared his views on education and the two worked closely to plan Tuskegee's future. Then he found an abandoned 100-acre farm for sale. The buildings on the property were small and not much better than the church shanty. Booker had no money, so the treasurer of the Hampton Institute gave him a personal loan.

A GUIDING PRINCIPLE

In a speech 20 years later, Booker outlined the philosophy that guided him from the beginning:

> **"The students of Tuskegee are taught the dignity of labor. There is a vast difference between being worked and working. Everybody who has to work is a**

slave; everybody who works because he wants to is a free man. . . . The greatest work that has yet been accomplished at Hampton and Tuskegee is that of teaching the Negro race that all labor is beautiful, dignified, and attractive. **"**

Booker quickly applied this philosophy. He and his students fixed the structures on the farm. He put the surrounding land into cultivation, a win-win-win situation. Students received training in farming, they grew crops they could eat, and the school sold what was left over to make money.

The next step was erecting a large building for offices and classrooms. Booker felt it was important to have a symbol to students and the surrounding community that the new school was here to stay. The price tag was steep: $6,000. This was a lot of money at the time. Booker got some of the money in small donations from the citizens of Tuskegee.

THE NECESSITY OF FUNDRAISING

By now it was apparent that fundraising was absolutely essential for the school's survival. Booker believed the primary source of money would be in the Northeast. The region had been a major source of opposition to slavery before the Civil War and still had a strong interest in promoting the welfare of blacks.

At first Olivia made the long trip to seek funds, but she wasn't strong enough to keep doing it. Booker had to assume the responsibility. Sometimes he would be gone for six to eight weeks at a time, spending many hours every day speaking and traveling from town to town. Typically he might make five or ten dollars at each stop.

In keeping with Booker's reliance on self-sufficiency, he introduced his students to making bricks. The school would need bricks for the buildings he planned. In addition, there was no brickyard in Tuskegee. The school would not only make money by selling bricks but also prove its worth to the white community by providing a necessary service.

Tuskegee students learned by doing; for example, constructing buildings, raising chickens, processing cotton and sewing, and stacking and drying hay. Booker's guiding principle was that work was dignified and useful. Students learned practical skills and helped themselves and the school by their labor.

BRICK BY BRICK BY BRICK

It proved easier to have the idea than to put it into practice. To begin with, brickmaking was hard, filthy work. Some students left school rather than continue with something they hated. Even harder was

"the task of making bricks with no money and no experience.... I had always supposed that brickmaking

was very simple, but I soon found out by bitter experience that it required special skill and knowledge.**" "**

Three times they built kilns to burn the bricks, and all three
times the kilns failed. There was no money for a fourth try. In
desperation, Booker **pawned** his watch. He received enough money
for a new kiln, which worked properly. The experience became an
important symbol of the school's ability to overcome adversity.

By the spring of 1882, Booker and Olivia had raised enough
money to begin construction of what would become Porter Hall.
It was named for a generous donor from Brooklyn, New York.
Students dug the foundation. When they laid the cornerstone,
Booker marveled that a building to educate blacks was about to be
raised in the heart of what had been slave owning territory:

**" "Sixteen years before that no Negro could be taught
from books without the teacher receiving the
condemnation of the law or of public sentiment—
when all this is considered, the scene that was
witnessed on that spring day at Tuskegee was a
remarkable one.** " "

That year Booker returned to Malden and married Fanny
Smith. She had been one of his students when he taught there.
The couple had a daughter, Portia, in 1883. But Fanny died of
unknown causes the following year.

LEARNING NEW SKILLS

By then the school was well established. The three-story Porter
Hall was the highest building in the area. More and more students
were attending.

But its very success created a problem. More students needed
more teachers and more buildings. In addition, Booker kept adding
new industries to teach to these students. Originally he had
emphasized basic skills such as carpentry and farming for men,
and housekeeping and sewing for women. Now students could

learn printing, nursing, and even broom-making. These trades all had one thing in common: they were useful in the white world.

The demands on Booker to raise money kept increasing, creating many sleepless nights for him:

> **❝Perhaps no one who has not gone through the experience, month after month, of trying to erect buildings and provide equipment for a school when no one knew where the money was to come from, can properly appreciate the difficulties under which we laboured.❞**

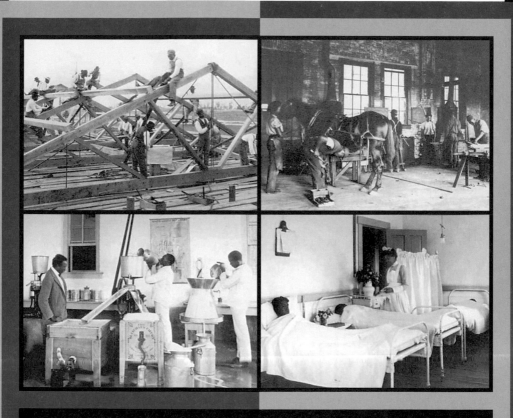

Many Tuskegee students learned more advanced skills—roof framing and woodwork, shoeing horses, pasteurizing milk, and nursing—that were useful in the white world. The school's success increased the demand for new buildings and teachers, which meant more fundraising efforts for Booker.

ANOTHER LOSS

Booker recovered from Fanny's death and married Olivia Davidson in 1885. They had two children, Booker Jr., born in 1887, and Ernest, born in 1889. Unfortunately, Olivia contracted a serious illness and died soon after Ernest's birth. "She literally wore herself out in her never ceasing efforts in behalf of the work that she so dearly loved," Booker wrote.

Her loss was devastating. Booker had sat by her bedside for weeks on end, completely neglecting fundraising. With the school about to close because of lack of money, Booker appealed to Armstrong. He responded with "all the money which he had saved for his own use," Booker wrote.

It is a tribute to Booker that he overcame the sorrow at losing two wives within four years and continued the school's upward progress. He celebrated Tuskegee's first decade in 1891. The campus now covered about 700 acres and the original 30 students had increased to more than 500. All the industries were humming along, providing for student needs and generating income for the school. In his mind, Booker had proven what blacks were capable of achieving.

Tuskegee Today

When Booker T. Washington died, Tuskegee Institute was firmly established. In the decades since then, it has continued to grow.

Tuskegee received nationwide attention in 1941 when it was chosen to host a special training program for black airmen. There was doubt that blacks could qualify as pilots. The men, who became famous as the Tuskegee Airmen, proved the doubters wrong. They compiled an outstanding combat record.

The school became a university in 1985. It is the only HBCU with an aerospace engineering school. Nearly three-quarters of black veterinarians nationwide have graduated from Tuskegee. Today over 3,000 students attend Tuskegee on a campus that includes 5,000 acres.

In 1892, Booker married Margaret Murray, a teacher at Tuskegee for several years. She had numerous responsibilities both at school and in the community in addition to taking care of Booker's three children. That was a huge help. As Booker noted,

Margaret Murray Washington was a teacher at Tuskegee who became Booker's third wife. He was devastated when his first two wives died young, leaving him with three small children. Fortunately he found happiness with Margaret, who was also active at Tuskegee and in their community.

"The thing in my life which brings me the keenest regret is that my work in connection with public affairs keeps me for so much of the time away from my family, where, of all places in the world, I delight to be."

Booker holds his niece Laura Murray as his two sons Ernest (left) and Booker T. Jr., look on. He loved his family, but he was sad that his school duties and fundraising trips often kept him away from them for long periods of time.

BIDDING FAREWELL TO ARMSTRONG

Booker had a bittersweet meeting in 1893 when Armstrong spent two months at Tuskegee. The general was paralyzed, yet in spite of his discomfort wanted to see Booker one more time. Armstrong died a few weeks after his departure, and his memory provided Booker with inspiration: "I resolved anew to devote myself more earnestly than ever to the cause which was so near his heart."

His resolution was somewhat easier because Tuskegee had expanded so much and its reputation had become greater. Now Booker was able to develop relationships with some of the country's wealthiest **philanthropists**. One of his most valuable associations was with Henry Rogers, whom Booker said he met about 1894. Rogers met Booker the day after he had given a speech in New York. He handed the astonished Booker ten $1,000-dollar bills.

Henry Rogers

Henry Rogers was born in 1840 in Fairhaven, Massachusetts. After graduating from high school, he worked as a grocery store clerk and railroad brakeman for several years. He carefully saved his money.

When Rogers was 21, he used his savings to open a small oil business. It became successful and Rogers eventually helped form Standard Oil, the nation's leading 19th century oil company. In relative terms, he was wealthier than Microsoft founder Bill Gates is now.

He had a reputation for being totally **ruthless** in business and yet kind to his friends. He donated considerable sums of money to worthy causes.

Henry Rogers died in 1909.

While he could never fully relax, Booker at least had the satisfaction of knowing that his hard work and dedication during the desperate early days had paid off. But he had no idea how high his fame and reputation were about to soar.

Chapter 4

Words Heard Around the Country

BY 1895, RELATIONS BETWEEN WHITES AND blacks in the South had grown much worse, and there was a dramatic upsurge in violence against blacks. On average a black man was lynched every three days. Black farms and schools were routinely torched. Blacks were often referred to in subhuman terms. An increasing number of **Jim Crow laws** limited their freedom and increased **segregation**. Some whites even wanted to ship blacks to Africa.

In this tense situation, Booker was invited to speak at the opening of the Cotton States and International Exposition in Atlanta, Georgia, on September 18, 1895. The Civil War had devastated the South's economy. The goal of the exposition was to demonstrate that the South had recovered. It showcased southern products and technologies, hoping to encourage outside investment and increase

Booker became a national figure when he spoke at the Atlanta Exposition in 1895. When he said that blacks needed to work hard and become better educated to fit into the white world, his speech found favor with both black and white listeners.

foreign trade. The exposition lasted for three months and attracted 800,000 people.

Booker had helped get congressional funding for the exposition:

"I said that the Atlanta Exposition would present an opportunity for both races to show what advance they had made since freedom, and would at the same time afford encouragement to them to make still greater progress."

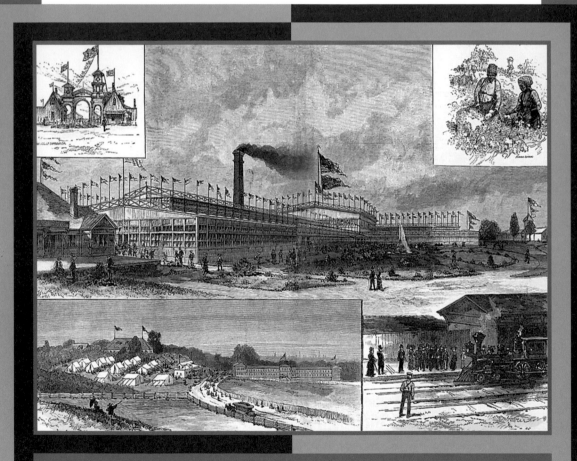

This illustration shows the Cotton States and International Exposition in Atlanta in 1895. Booker was honored to be asked to speak there because he was the first black man invited to appear on the same stage with white men and women.

The organizers thought it would be a good public relations move to have a black speaker. Booker was the obvious choice. He was keenly aware of the significance:

❝This was the first time in the entire history of the Negro that a member of my race had been asked to speak from the same platform with white Southern men and women on any important National occasion.❞

Booker knew his words would be carefully examined. He went over and over what he would say. Even with all his practice, Booker barely slept the night before the speech.

"CAST DOWN YOUR BUCKET"

He began by thanking the exposition's directors for allowing him to speak. Then he told a story. A ship at sea has run out of water. When another vessel appears, the first ship signals its problem. "Cast down your bucket where you are," replies the other. The first vessel is near the mouth of the Amazon River. The bucket comes up filled with fresh water.

The story had several meanings. He expressed one when he urged blacks to "cast [the bucket] down in making friends in every manly way of the people of all races by whom we are surrounded." In other words, make every effort to get along with whites.

Another was to "cast it down in agriculture, mechanics, in commerce, in domestic service, and in the professions. . . . Our greatest danger is that in the great leap from slavery to freedom we may overlook the fact that the masses of us are to live by the productions of our hands." This was clear advice to take up trades that would benefit whites.

The third meaning was directed at whites, asking them to cast their bucket "down among the eight millions of Negroes whose habits you know . . . the same people who have, without strikes and labour wars, tilled your fields, cleared your forests, builded your railroads and cities, and brought forth treasures from the bowels of the earth."

POINTING OUT THE POSITIVE

Booker also emphasized the good qualities of blacks—loyal, law-abiding, peaceful—in an effort to counter prevailing ideas among whites that blacks were lazy, immoral, shiftless, and inclined to crime.

Soon he reached what would be the most remembered part of his speech. He held up his right hand and said,

> **"In all things that are purely social we can be as separate as the fingers, yet one as the hand in all things essential to mutual progress."**

As he spoke, he spread his fingers apart, then closed them into a fist. Near the end, he added his opinion that

> **"The wisest among my race understand that the agitation of questions of social equality is the extremest folly, and that progress in the enjoyment of all the privileges that will come to us must be the result of severe and constant struggle rather than of artificial forcing."**

Here Booker was saying that blacks had to give up the struggle for civil rights. Instead, they needed to focus their efforts on working hard and becoming better educated. At some future point, whites would grant them those rights.

A PRACTICAL APPROACH

In this respect, Booker felt he was being practical. If he called for blacks to struggle against their oppressive conditions, it might incite a violent backlash. And he genuinely believed that the two races could eventually live in harmony.

As soon as soon as he finished speaking, Georgia governor Rufus Bullock rushed over to shake his hand—a real rarity in black-white relations. The audience was on its feet, applauding and cheering. The enthusiasm continued on as Booker left the

Booker speaks at the Atlanta exposition, September 18, 1895. He pointed out the positive attributes of black people, in contrast to some whites' beliefs that blacks were lazy and ignorant. Booker also emphasized that the races needed to work together toward the betterment of society.

stage: "I received so many and such hearty congratulations that I found it difficult to get out of the building."

Whites were especially happy. Booker said that blacks would remain second-class citizens, while providing a source of relatively inexpensive labor. Many thought that Booker's being half-white accounted for the intelligence he had shown in the speech.

Many blacks also approved. "No word uttered by a colored man during the past 20 years will go farther and do more to set us right in public opinion," said a black lawyer. A young college professor named W.E.B. Du Bois said the speech was "the basis of a real settlement between whites and blacks in the South."

Du Bois—and many other blacks—would eventually change their minds about the speech. They would call it the Atlanta Compromise. Booker would be harshly criticized.

W.E.B. Du Bois, a leader in the fight for racial equality, works in his office. In his many books, he constantly spoke out about the need for black advancement. Du Bois criticized Booker for compromising with whites instead of stressing black equality.

W.E.B. Du Bois

William Edward Burghardt Du Bois was born in Massachusetts in 1868 and graduated from Fisk University in Tennessee in 1888. He became the first black man to earn a Ph.D. degree from Harvard University and taught college for many years.

Du Bois helped found the National Association for the Advancement of Colored People (NAACP) in 1909. He served as editor of *The Crisis*, the organization's monthly magazine, for 25 years. He ran for the U.S. Senate in 1952. During his life, he wrote many books and continually spoke out in favor of black advancements.

He died in the African country of Ghana in 1963.

TAKING ON MORE RESPONSIBILITY

That was in the future. The timing of the speech was prophetic. Frederick Douglass, the former slave who had been the most prominent spokesman for blacks for many years, had died several months earlier. Up that point, no one had emerged to take his place.

Booker's speech catapulted him into the spotlight and was widely reprinted. One reporter, after calling Booker the "Negro Moses," added that he "must rank from this time forth as the foremost man of his race in America."

Timothy Fortune, editor of the black newspaper *New York Age*, said,

"It looks as if you are our Douglass. You are the best equipped of the lot of us to be the single figure ahead of the procession."

Booker T. Washington was now a national figure. Up to this point, he had been responsible for the welfare of several hundred students at Tuskegee. Almost overnight, his responsibilities had expanded to cover the eight million blacks to whom he referred in his speech.

One thing was clear. Booker's life would never be the same.

Booker T. Washington's Legacy

IN THE AFTERMATH OF THE ATLANTA SPEECH, donations to Tuskegee increased. But there never seemed to be enough money. One reason was that Booker was always looking to expand. In 1896 he created an agricultural school at Tuskegee. Noted black scientist George Washington Carver served as the school's head.

STILL OPTIMISTIC

That same year Booker received an honorary masters degree from Harvard. It was the first time a black man had received such an honor. During his acceptance speech, Booker repeated his optimism about racial progress:

> "We are coming up, and with proper habits, intelligence and property, there is no power on earth that can permanently stay our progress."

Booker poses with his wealthy white friends and donors and the Tuskegee Institute faculty. After his speech in Atlanta, donations to Tuskegee increased. The school had become a great institution of black education, but Booker was exhausted by his constant fundraising efforts.

This honor came from the white world. In the black world, Booker was having problems. Not long after the Atlanta speech, black educator John Hope had written, "I regard it as cowardly and dishonest for any of our colored men to tell white people or colored people that we are not struggling for equality."

Dealing with these and other criticisms, his much higher public profile, and continuous fundraising exhausted Booker. His friends persuaded him to take a vacation in 1899 and visit Europe. He thoroughly enjoyed the trip, during which he met many famous people and even had tea with Queen Victoria of England. The following year Booker created the National Negro Business League to help promote black businessmen.

Booker (right) works in his office at Tuskegee. In 1900 he started writing books about his life. His second book, *Up From Slavery* is considered a classic in black literature. He was also awarded honorary degrees, in recognition of his devotion to educating black students.

BECOMING AN AUTHOR

He also began publishing. His first book, *The Story of My Life and Work*, didn't do well when it came out in 1900. The following year he published *Up From Slavery*. The book did considerably better and has become a classic of black literature. The final pages expressed Booker's optimism about ultimate racial harmony:

> **"Despite superficial and temporary signs which might lead one to entertain a contrary opinion, there was never a time when I felt more hopeful for the race than I do at the present."**

Later that year, Dartmouth College in New Hampshire awarded him an honorary doctorate degree. For the rest of his life, he would often be referred to as "Dr. Washington." In conferring the degree, the school said,

> **"Mr. Washington is representative of the capability of his race, and America may well hearken to the voice of one who has devoted his life to the cause of his distressed people with such tremendous energy, and indomitable perseverance."**

DINNER WITH THE PRESIDENT

In October, 1901 President Theodore Roosevelt invited Booker to dinner at the White House, the first time such an invitation had been extended to a black man. Southern whites were outraged. They believed Roosevelt was encouraging racial equality. Despite the objections, the invitation further raised Booker's profile among many other whites.

Opposition was increasing within the black community. In 1903 W.E.B. Du Bois wrote *The Souls of Black Folk*. One chapter criticized Booker. Du Bois thought Booker was too accommodating to whites. He also accused him of trying to silence blacks who disagreed with him. He said Booker used his influence to **suppress** negative articles about him in the black press.

The NAACP was founded in 1909. Organizers invited Booker but he chose not to attend. The organization soon became the leading **advocacy** group for blacks. Booker's influence began to fade.

CONTINUING HIS HEAVY WORKLOAD

Yet he wouldn't stop. He worked just as hard as ever at Tuskegee, helping the school continue to expand and continuing his fund-raising. He also wrote three more books, *The Story of the Negro* in 1909, *My Larger Education* in 1911, and *The Man Farthest Down* the following year.

In 1912 he convinced philanthropist Julius Rosenwald to serve on the Tuskegee board of directors. Rosenwald soon began donating money to build more black schools in the South.

Julius Rosenwald and Rosenwald Schools

Julius Rosenwald was born in Illinois in 1862 and moved to New York as a teenager to learn the clothing trade. He founded a clothing company that became a principal supplier to Sears, Roebuck and Company.

Later he became president of Sears. The company thrived under his direction and Rosenwald became very wealthy.

He donated much of his wealth. He gave $5 million to found the Museum of Science and Industry in Chicago.

He is most famous for the Rosenwald Fund, which provided millions of dollars for schools and colleges across the United States. He was especially concerned with the poor condition of black education in rural areas. The fund granted money to build more than 5,000 schools for rural black children in southern states. By the early 1930s, more than one-third of these youngsters were being educated in Rosenwald Schools.

That same year Woodrow Wilson was elected President. Wilson immediately began to rigidly segregate the government. He also made it clear that he had no interest in seeking Booker's advice, which continued his decline in influence.

Yet to many blacks, Booker was still an inspiring figure. When he spoke in New Orleans, a very old woman who had spent many years as a slave came with one goal in mind. She said, "Whar Booker? Whar Booker? I want to see Booker."

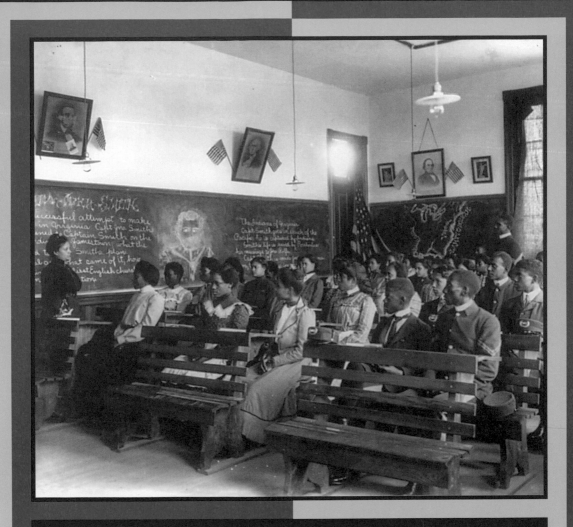

Tuskegee students listen to their teacher. Booker kept working to help the school expand. He was always trying to interest philanthropists in Tuskegee, and his fundraising efforts didn't stop until the day he died.

RAISING HIS VOICE

By this time Booker had begun speaking out more forcefully against injustice. In a pamphlet called "Is the Negro Having a Fair Chance," he noted numerous instances in which blacks suffered unequal treatment in comparison to whites. Education was one:

"The negro in the South should feel that he is unfairly treated when he has, as is often true in the country districts, either no school at all, or one with a term of no more than four or five months, taught in the wreck of a log-cabin and by a teacher who is paid about half the price of a first-class convict."

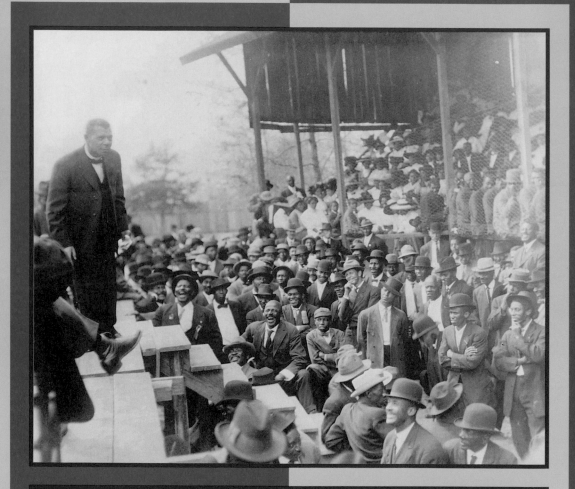

A crowd reacts to Booker's speech. In his later years, Booker began to speak out more forcefully against racial inequality. He said that many blacks still did not receive an adequate education, which was the key to success for people of all races.

Not everything Booker did was public knowledge. In secret, he financed several legal challenges to southern policies of segregation.

But the long years of struggle were taking their toll. Booker was clearly in failing health. Yet he continued to work. In 1892 he had begun the annual Tuskegee Negro Conferences, which provided advice and inspiration to black farmers. In 1914 he broadened their scope to include health care for blacks.

The following year he helped promote National Negro Health Week. He also led a successful fight against a bill in Congress that would have forbidden anyone of African descent from coming to the United States.

HIS FINAL DAYS

Booker's health grew even worse. In early November 1915 he was in New York, raising funds for Tuskegee. He fell ill and was hospitalized. Realizing he was dying, he had one final trip to make:

> **"I was born in the South, have lived all my life in the South, and expect to die and be buried in the South."**

In considerable pain, Booker boarded a train and set out for Tuskegee. He died a few hours after his arrival, in the early morning of November 14.

Tributes poured in. Madame C. J. Walker, the country's first successful black businesswoman, called him "the greatest man America ever knew." Former president Theodore Roosevelt said,

> **"He was one of the distinguished citizens of the United States, a man who rendered greater service to his race than had ever been rendered by any one else."**

Julius Rosenwald added,

> **"The injustices he was made to suffer never embittered him. . . . His life enriched not only this country but the entire world."**

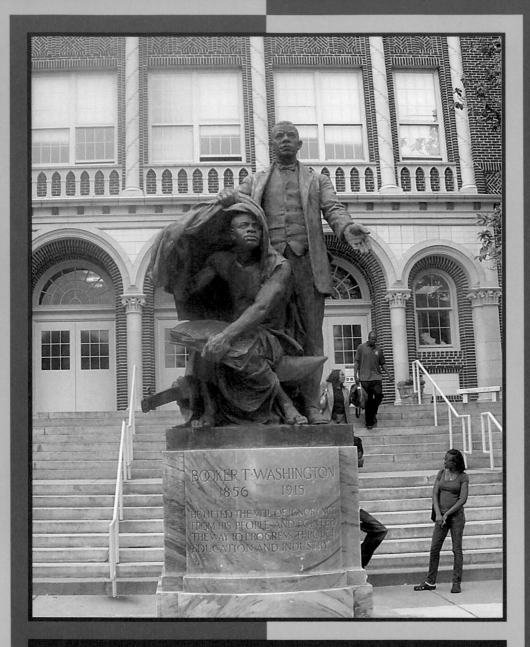

Booker's image appears on a statue in front of a high school named after him in Atlanta. The statue depicts Booker lifting the "veil of ignorance" from a black man through his passion for education. His dedication to that cause is the lasting legacy of one of the most important educators in American history.

NEVER TO BE FORGOTTEN

Booker's name and fame live on in many ways. Statues depicting Booker appear at both Hampton and Tuskegee. Many schools in the United States bear his name. Booker was the first black whose image appeared on a postage stamp. And of course, there is Tuskegee University.

SS *Booker T. Washington*

One of Booker's most interesting honors came in 1942 when the Liberty ship SS *Booker T. Washington* was launched. Liberty ships carried vital cargoes during World War II. More than 2,700 were built. The *Booker T. Washington* was the first of 18 named after blacks. Famed black opera singer Marian Anderson christened the vessel.

The captain of the ship was Hugh Mulzac, who became the first black to command an ocean-going vessel. Plans called for an all-black crew. Mulzac refused to sail unless the crew was integrated. The ship's crew eventually had 18 different nationalities.

The vessel made 22 round trips during the war. It was scrapped in 1969.

Given the context of his time, Booker's accomplishments were considerable. He achieved his greatest fame at the moment of the greatest danger for blacks. He did what he felt he could do within those limitations.

There can be no doubt about his honest and complete dedication to the cause of black education. He worked tirelessly from the moment he arrived at Tuskegee in 1881 till his last day. He was clearly the foremost black educator of his time, and one of the most important in all of U.S. history.

1856 Born into slavery on a plantation in Virginia.

1865 Moves with family to Malden, West Virginia, after end of Civil War.

1872 Enters Hampton Normal and Agricultural Institute in Hampton, Virginia.

1875 Graduates from Hampton.

Begins teaching in Malden.

1878 Enters Wayland Baptist Theological Seminary.

1879 Begins teaching at Hampton.

1881 Is appointed principal of Tuskegee Normal and Industrial Institute in Tuskegee, Alabama.

1882 Constructs first building on Tuskegee campus.

Marries Fanny Smith.

1883 Daughter Portia is born.

1884 Wife Fanny dies.

1885 Tuskegee has its first graduating class.

Booker marries Olivia Davidson.

1887 Son Booker T. Washington Jr. is born.

1889 Son Ernest is born.

Wife Olivia dies.

1892 Marries Margaret Murray.

First Tuskegee Negro Conference is held.

1895 Delivers "Atlanta Compromise" speech on September 18 at the Cotton States and International Exposition in Atlanta, Georgia.

1896 Invites George Washington Carver to form a department of agriculture at Tuskegee.

1899   Takes European vacation.

1901   Publishes *Up from Slavery*.

Is invited by President Theodore Roosevelt to the White House for dinner on October 6.

1903   Begins feud with W.E.B. Du Bois after *The Souls of Black Folk* Is published.

Receives $600,000 donation from Andrew Carnegie.

1909   Declines invitation to help found the National Association for the Advancement of Colored People (NAACP).

1912   Persuades philanthropist Julius Rosenwald to join Tuskegee board of trustees.

1915   Sponsors National Negro Health Week.

Dies in Tuskegee on November 14.

1875 Delivers address at his Hampton Institute graduation.

1879 Invited to give commencement address at Hampton Institute.

1896 Receives honorary masters degree from Harvard University.

1899 Invited to tea by Queen Victoria of England.

1900 Founds and becomes first president of National Negro Business League.

Publishes *The Story of My Life and Work*.

1901 Publishes *Up from Slavery*, his autobiography.

Receives honorary doctorate of laws degree from Dartmouth College.

Receives invitation from President Theodore Roosevelt to dine at the White House.

1908 Is honored by government of Liberia with Order of African Redemption.

1909 Publishes *The Story of the Negro*.

1911 Publishes *My Larger Education: Chapters from My Experience*.

1912 Publishes *The Man Farthest Down*.

1916 Memorial service to honor Booker T. Washington is held in Carnegie Hall in New York City.

1922 Tuskegee Institute dedicates "Lifting the Veil" statue of Booker T. Washington.

1929 Booker Washington Institute is founded in Liberia as the country's first vocational and agricultural school.

1934 Tuskegee president Robert Moton sets up tour by two black aviators in aircraft called the *Booker T. Washington*.

1940 Becomes first black American whose image appears on a postage stamp, as part of Famous American Educators series.

1941 Black poet Langston Hughes writes "The Ballad of Booker T."

1942   SS *Booker T. Washington* becomes the first Liberty ship to be named for a black American.

1945   Elected to Hall of Fame of Great Americans on campus of City University of New York.

1946   Becomes first black American whose image appears on a coin.

1956   U.S. postage stamp shows image of a slave cabin similar to the one in which Booker was born to honor the 100th anniversary of his birth.

Booker T. Washington National Monument in Virginia opens.

1965   The Tuskegee campus is designated as a national historic site.

1984   Hampton University dedicates Booker T. Washington memorial.

2002   Included in book *100 Greatest African Americans*, by Molefi Kete Asante.

abolishing—doing away with, eliminating.

advocacy—supporting or encouraging a cause.

condemnation—blame, criticism.

dilapidated—run-down, badly needing repair.

engrafted—fastened, imposed.

Jim Crow laws—laws that discriminated against blacks, usually by forcing them to use separate and lower quality facilities.

mulatto—person of mixed white and black ancestry.

orator—a very good public speaker.

pawned—gave an object as security in exchange for a loan.

philanthropists—wealthy people who donate large sums of money to worthy causes.

ratified—approved, accepted.

ruthless—having no pity or mercy.

segregation—separation of whites and blacks, often enforced by law.

sloven—showing little or no concern for personal appearance; sloppy.

suppress—put down.

tangible—something that can be touched.

Books

Keller, Kristin Thoennes. *Booker T. Washington: Innovative Educator* (Signature Lives: Modern America series). Mankato, Minnesota: Compass Point Books, 2007.

Schraff, Anne E. *Booker T. Washington: "Character Is Power"* (African-American Biography Library). Berkeley Heights, New Jersey: Enslow, 2006.

Schroeder, Alan and Anne Beier. *Booker T. Washington: Educator And Racial Spokesman* (Black Americans of Achievement). Philadelphia: Chelsea House, 2005.

Swain, Gwyneth. *A Hunger For Learning: A Story About Booker T. Washington* (Creative Minds Biographies). Minneapolis, Minnesota: Lerner, 2005.

Wukovits, John F. *Booker T. Washington and Entrepreneurship* (Lucent Library of Black History). San Diego, California: Lucent Books, 2008.

Web Sites

http://www.celebratebookert.org/
This Web Site focuses on values that Booker T. Washington held and sought to instill in his students and in others.

http://www.nps.gov/bowa/index.htm
This guide to Booker T. Washington National Monument in Virginia includes visitor information, biography, photos, activities.

http://memory.loc.gov/ammem/aaohtml/exhibit/aopart6.html
"The Booker T. Washington Era" is part of Library of Congress *The African American Odyssey: A Quest for Full Citizenship* Exhibition and includes brief descriptions of numerous aspects of black culture during Booker T. Washington's lifetime.

http://www.tuskegeeairmen.org/
This Web site offers complete information about Tuskegee airmen, including history and pictures.

PICTURE CREDITS

ABOUT THE AUTHOR

Jim Whiting has written more than 100 children's non-fiction books and edited well over 150 more during an especially diverse writing career. He published *Northwest Runner* magazine for more than 17 years. His other credits include advising a national award-winning high school newspaper, sports editor for the *Bainbridge Island Review*, event and venue write-ups and photography for American Online, articles in dozens of magazines, light verse in the *Saturday Evening Post*, the first piece of original fiction to appear in *Runner's World*, and official photographer for the Antarctica Marathon. His other Mason Crest titles include *American Idol Judges*, *Troy Polamalu*, *David Beckham*, *Hilary Duff*, and *Mandy Moore*.